The Imprisoned Splendor

Discovering Your
Spiritual Self

The Imprisoned Splendor

Discovering Your Spiritual Self

Robert A. Wasner

with Colleen Wasner and David Starke

MALAMALAMA PRESS
Kailua, Hawaii

The Imprisoned Splendor
Discovering Your Spiritual Self

Copyright © 1996 by Robert A. Wasner

For information, please contact:
Malamalama Press
109 Hekili Street
Kailua, HI 96734
(800) 852-7140

Printed in the United States of America

First Printing - September 1996

Cover photograph by
Thomas Mark deHarne

ISBN 0-9654023-0-4   (pbk.)
LC Number 96-094720

Dedication

I dedicate this book to
the imprisoned splendor
within each of us.
May we let it escape!

Acknowledgments

I wish to give a heartfelt "Thank You!" to my daughter, Colleen and her partner, David Starke, who labored for months over this manuscript editing and proofreading. I am quite convinced that it would never have happened if it were not for them.

I wish also to thank my wife, Mary June, who has given me support all along the way. And a special thanks to Wally Amos and John Strickland, who read the manuscript and encouraged me in my quest.

Thank you Des and Jean deLacy-Bourke, for your steadfast moral support and faithful friendship throughout the years.

Robert A. Wasner
Kailua, Hawaii

Table of Contents

Foreword

𝔍 first heard of the Reverend Robert "Bob" Wasner about thirty years ago. My brother, upon returning home from the hospital after a near fatal automobile accident, informed me that he had just met our new minister. "What's he like?" I asked. "He's nice." Next Sunday, I met Bob and found that my brother was right. But Bob was more than just nice, he was (and remains) an inspiration to me. I treasure the time I spent with him. Nearly ten years later, as a young seminary student, I let Bob in on a secret: he had been the one to inspire me to be a minister. I am forever grateful for his inspiration and deeply honored to write the foreword for his book.

In the three decades that I have known Bob I have found him to be a treasure trove of useful information on the Bible, metaphysics, history, archaeology, counseling, sociology, anthropology, politics, and more. I am constantly amazed at how much inner wisdom he possesses, how much worldly knowledge he has acquired, and how sensitively he ministers to those around him.

I find this work to be an opulent tapestry of profound, universal, spiritual laws. These deep, transformative truths are made understandable and practical through the Reverend Wasner's masterful weaving of precepts, scripture, commentary, and storytelling.

The great New England transcendentalist, Ralph Waldo Emerson, once said, "What you are thunders so loudly that I cannot hear what you are saying to the contrary." I am proud to say that what Reverend Wasner has to say is congruent with who he is. I am privileged to know the author of this book, and I am certain that all who read it will also feel privileged to know my friend and mentor, Bob Wasner.

Reverend John Strickland
Senior Minister, Unity Church of
Hawaii
Former Director of Silent Unity and
Vice-President of Unity School
of Christianity

Preface

As a rule the leading idea of a new religion comes from the symbolism of the religion that preceded it. For instance, the leading idea of a new religion to follow the Christian age would be that everyone is the Christ.
Carl Jung, The Visions Seminars

I remember in 1954 watching the prototype of the Boeing 707, a plane that would soon revolutionize jet aircraft, being taken out and flown over Lake Washington in Seattle during the Gold Cup hydroplane races. This was the first time the 707 had ever been publicly displayed.

Tex Johnson, the chief test pilot for Boeing, was supposed to simply fly down to the end of the lake, turn around, and fly back. Instead, Tex brought the new 707 so close to the water that it blew a rooster tail, just like the hydroplanes. This was not a small craft at all, but a passenger plane. Everyone witnessing this was stunned. Then, as if that wasn't enough, Johnson made a steep climb and started back across the lake, soon shocking the crowd further by doing three barrel rolls! As we all stood in disbelief, we began to realize that this prototype represented a whole new generation of aircraft.

In the same way, Jesus was the prototype for the new humanity.   One statement that Jesus made was, " ...the works that I do you shall do also; *and greater works than these shall you do.*"   He was setting the example for a transformed existence.   Jesus showed clearly that we are, each and every one of us, *divine.*

Many of us might be going through some very unusual changes right now.   Some of these changes may shake us up and some might seem to be coming from our innermost core. These reflective, synchronistic, emotional, revelatory experiences are the sensations we experience when we open up to our own spiritual transformation.   So often we have forgotten that we truly are spiritual beings. The lines of poet Robert Browning can show us so clearly what we are, and remind us well:

No matter what you may believe
There is an inmost center in us all
Where truth abides in fullness
And to know consist in opening out a way
Whence the imprisoned splendor
may escape
Rather than effecting entry
For a light supposed to be without.

While we are physical, mental, emotional and spiritual, it is only from our spiritual selves that growth and change can take place. True change must come from deep within the center of our being. Our spiritual self is like the butterfly emerging from the cocoon.

In this book there will be references to *Jesus* and *Christ*. The two are not exactly the same. Jesus was a man of Nazareth who taught a small group of followers some 2,000 years ago. Christ is that portion of divinity which is in everyone. Jesus fully lived from that divine essence, his spiritual self. When he taught, he was setting an example of what we all may become, *if we acknowledge and live by our spiritual source.*

The imprisoned splendor is there, in each and every one of us, no matter what we may believe. For that splendor is far more than just what we think and how we act and how we may or may not feel. In us, each and every one of us, abides the fullness of truth: that we are all from the same source.

Jesus spoke, but more importantly, lived, as the example of a humanity that recognizes and acknowledges that our essence is Spirit. It is time now for *opening out a way, whence the imprisoned splendor may escape.* It is time now also to soar.

1

The Spiritual Law of Consciousness

To forgive everybody for everything at
all times, regardless of circumstances,
is the first step toward complete emancipation.
Christian Daa Larson

Centuries ago, in the Punjab of India, there lived a man named Nanak, who would later found Sikhism. Nanak, a devoutly religious man, would join the crowd to bow and pray to the West, facing Mecca, five times every day.

One day, when Nanak went out to pray with hundreds of other faithful, he noticed a sharp stone protruding from the ground where he was to bow his head. Nanak turned then, so that his face would be safe when he bowed, the jagged stone now at his feet. Soon, however, a guard came by and said angrily, "You blaspheme God!" Nanak replied, "How is this?" The guard said, "Your feet are pointing in the direction of God!" "Then, sir," Nanak answered, "as you wish. Show me where God is not, and I shall place my feet in that direction."

Nanak, like the old rhyme, *could not find a spot where God is not*. He was experiencing the loving source of creation as inherent in all things. These insights were gained through an expanded consciousness, which refers ultimately to our own awareness of the nature of Spirit.

As we allow our perceptions to expand, we increase our sensitivity to the divine. The more expanded the vistas, the more sacred the experience becomes for the experiencer. Of course, everything is holy, always. Our problem is much simpler than what the existentialists determined. God is not dead, but we may have let our consciousness go numb, and so find ourselves desensitized to the nature of life itself. This happens when we become alienated from universal principles.

In our lives, there are many human laws that we adhere to, partly to avoid chaos, and partly to establish a harmony with one another. There are physical laws, such as gravity or inertia, that we are subject to. There are also *spiritual* laws that, always, we are working with. Some of these laws we may not know by any certain name. They are spiritual principles that are operative in the world; the names given here for each law attempt to sum up the specific aspect that we are looking at.

Many times I've heard people say things like, "I've sure had lots of misery in my life because I've broken so many of those spiritual laws." But we don't have misery in our lives because we have broken any spiritual laws. We have misery in our lives because we have broken *ourselves*, trying to break spiritual laws.

If a law is spiritual, we're not going to break it. These spiritual laws exist, and they are going to continue to exist, regardless of what we do about them. To talk of breaking spiritual laws is like saying, "I've really gotten a lot of bruises, breaking the law of gravity." We didn't break the law of gravity: the law of gravity was operating perfectly, and that's why we got the bruises. The same is true with the spiritual laws in our lives.

In this first chapter, we will look at the Spiritual Law of Consciousness. The Law of Consciousness is probably best expressed by Jesus in the Lord's Prayer: *"Forgive us our debts, as we also have forgiven our debtors."* How many times have we said that line and how many times have we heard others say it? But how many times have we heard into what the principle is *behind* that statement? It's very subtle, but very powerful, because the lines from that prayer say, "We can only *have in our lives* that which we're willing to *be*."

In translating the Lord's Prayer, Aramaic linguists have found that what Jesus actually said was closer to, "Thou hast forgiven my debts *as I have been willing* to forgive the debts of others." Only to the degree that we are willing to be forgiving to the world, are we going to feel forgiveness within ourselves. We can only have that forgiveness because we have been willing to *be* forgiving. We can only have that which we are willing to be.

You can't really have love unless you are willing to be loving.   You cannot have forgiveness unless you are willing to be forgiving.   This issue of forgiveness relates to the feeling of guilt as well.   Guilt can be the price we pay for not being forgiving out in the world.   If we are not forgiving of all the things that have happened to us, too often we *compensate for this lack of forgiveness by feeling guilty* about all the things that we do. But if we are truly forgiving, and if we are truly loving to all whom we encounter and to all situations that arise in our lives, then we are not going to feel guilty within ourselves.

So guilt becomes a trade-off, you see, as far as experiencing guilt and still holding un-forgiveness.   There is no need for guilt if we are being as loving and as forgiving as we are able to be.   If we are truly going to be forgiving, and this includes forgiving *ourselves*, then we're going to have forgiveness in our lives.   This is the only way that we can have it.   By *being* it.

The Law of Consciousness is a practical principle.   Even on a *physical* level it is unhealthy not to forgive, so we can imagine how it must affect the psyche.   Malice, resentment, and non-forgiveness are just some of the emotions that can chip away at our own well-being, and if we let them, they will readily lead us from our inner path.   Remember that always there is someone in what seems to be a better position than you and always, someone worse off.   "Let it go" is good folk wisdom.   It can be very hard to do this sometimes, because letting go is *too easy.* If people had to spend a lot of money and do something exotic and complicated, they might have more confidence in the effectiveness of *letting go.* We may not understand a situation or a person, but we *can know* that by listening to that inner voice we all have, we will be guided in loving action, and we will find peace where before there was only pain.

When we treat a situation with forgiveness, that loving action always seeks to alleviate the deepest suffering. Sometimes in life we can get confused and create our own suffering, feeling or thinking that suffering is somehow "necessary." Sometimes we can create our own suffering or become a part of someone else's created suffering by our own ignorance, or by avoiding honest and loving attention to the situation. So we need to come back to our center when responding to *all* the circumstances we may find ourselves in.

It is wonderful to see the tremendous changes that take place when people first come into an awareness of some of these spiritual principles. We find that amazing changes take place. I think of the first time that I heard some of these spiritual laws and what a great difference it made in my life. I went out and I was really attempting to be positive, and to watch the words that I spoke. I was getting away from all of the "can'ts" and all of the "I trieds" and all of the "shoulds" and all those other blocking words in our lives. Next, I was starting new habits and saying things like, "I'm willing" and "I'm open" and "I can."   I began being positive and focusing in on the positive aspects of my life.

The interesting thing is, that in the beginning part of touching these principles, marvelous things happened in my life. I saw all sorts of doors of good being opened.

I found myself in those early days focusing on praying, meditating, visualizing, tithing, and doing all these various things...and they worked!   They worked and it was wonderful!   What happened, however, after a period of time, was that it seemed that these things didn't work quite as well. I bet many of you have experienced this also. I wondered, "Why?" I thought, "How come these principles don't work as well now as they used to?"

Not too long ago a man came up to me and said, "I haven't been to your services for awhile.   You know, when I first started attending, everything began going great.   My life was really working.   I practiced those principles and boy did they work!"   Then he said, "Now I'm kinda bored.   I'm sorta depressed because these things don't seem to work anymore."

In answering this problem, I have to say that it's not that the principles don't work anymore, it's that we have forgotten to *be* them. We have substituted, for example, our *knowledge* of these principles for the actual *practice* of them. This is quite simple to do, too simple. We can *know* all about prayer, so that when something comes up we think about our knowledge of prayer, instead of praying. Some of us seem to shift spiritual principles over to the left side of our brain. We start rationalizing and reflecting, rather than letting these principles become part of the process of our lives. Instead, we need to get in touch with that quiet and still part of us, that inner voice that is in touch with the deepest truths of our being.

When we pray, we are getting in touch with the intuitive part of ourselves that is of the emotions, of the feelings. Often, we may move away from our intuitive side. We need to move back to our inner self, and learn to trust its wisdom. It seems easy to substitute all that we *know* about truth for the practice of truth. Once we are living these principles for awhile and using them, it is especially easy to substitute what we know about spiritual law instead of living through love.

I'm always amazed at seeing people who embrace these principles and start applying them right away. These principles begin working wonderfully in their lives. I see people making new relationships in their lives, and I see them happier and healthier. I see new opportunities and possibilities arising in totally unexpected ways. But I also see that it is so easy to get into a rut.

And isn't it easy to get stuck, and to forget to put these principles into our daily practice? In terms of getting into a rut, I think about an old story that illustrates this idea.

There was a man who left a tavern one evening after he'd had too much to drink. As he was wandering home, he crossed through a cemetery. There was a newly opened grave right in the man's path, and the unfortunate fellow tumbled into it.

It had rained earlier that evening, and the sides of the grave pit were very slippery. The man, after getting to his feet, tried again and again to climb up the earthen walls of the hole, but he could not get out. Finally, he determined that there was just no way he could get out. He had tried and tried and had only wound up muddy and tired. So he crawled into a corner and went to sleep.

About an hour later, another man coming from the same tavern was wandering through the cemetery, very drunk, and he fell into that same hole.

The first man was still in a corner of the grave, but he remained silent. He just watched the shadowy figure of the new arrival trying to climb out, over and over again. Finally, he looked at the man, who was wheezing from exhaustion, and said, "You can't get out of here." *But he did!*

Now, you can say that's really motivation, but whatever it is, we find it's uncanny what brings out the positive parts of us at times, and allows us to awaken ourselves out of any ruts we have fallen into. This means tapping into a higher wellspring of potential than we had ever before realized.

When Jesus talked about 'becoming as children,' he meant for us to go back to the very center of ourselves. This involves going beyond our ordinary, limited mind and transcending the barriers that we've built up within. Jesus was emphasizing here the direct experience and wonder of life, our need to touch our hearts.

What a difference it would make if, this week, we forgot everything that we *knew* about spiritual principles and we started over again and said, "I can only *have* that which I am willing to *be*." What a difference it would make in our lives, and those around us, if we began applying this spiritual law.

The Law of Consciousness teaches that *if I want things to work out positively in my life, then I've got to create the space for it.* I create the space for it by being positive. So I'm going to watch what I say, and I'm going to really look at the words I use. I'm going to watch the way I'm looking at things, and the way that I'm seeing both my life and other people.

If the imprisoned splendor is going to unfold into our lives, then we have to create the space for it. So I'm going to be peaceful, thereby creating the space for peace in my life. I'm going to be forgiving of others, and I'm going to create a space for myself to have a feeling of forgiveness. I'm going to give because I know it opens up a channel that allows me to have wider vision and more abundance in my life.

If we were to do these things, what would happen? We would be back to where we'd see these spiritual laws working and we wouldn't find ourselves bored.   We wouldn't find ourselves depressed.   We wouldn't find this feeling that, "Oh, these things used to work, but they don't work as well now." We need to live with these principles fully, and not let the "knowledge" of love be a substitute for *being* loving.

Back when I first started in the ministry, I thought that the real purpose of Unity was to do itself out of business.   That is, to get everybody so self-reliant that we didn't have to be here.

But that's a real idealistic belief, because every one of us has things that happen each week so that we have the need of coming together and reaffirming these spiritual truths. Once again, these truths are so simple, they're *too* simple. If they were more complicated, we would probably do much better with them. But they are so simple that we need to come together to remind ourselves of the simplicity, and to remind ourselves to *practice* these truths.

There's an old saying that goes, "You've got to walk your talk," which means that you've got to live what you're talking about. If you don't do that, life doesn't mean anything. It doesn't mean anything as to how other people view us, and it doesn't mean anything to us, because the internal part of us is in conflict then with the external part of us. When you 'walk your talk,' you are being true to yourself.

The songwriter Johnny Mercer was a good example of this. You might remember his lyric, "You've got to accentuate the positive." He wrote some of the most positive lyrics that I've ever heard.

Johnny Mercer's father, who evidently was a very kind person, borrowed a good deal of money and had debts with everyone in Savannah. A friend of mine who knew the Mercer family told me that when Johnny Mercer's father passed away, there were debts all over that his father had incurred.

When Johnny Mercer made some money from a few of the early songs he wrote, he paid off every single debt of his father's. It would have been quite easy for him to say, "Well, those were my father's debts, they aren't mine." But again, he walked his talk. He lived what he believed. Johnny Mercer did not just write words about "accentuating the positive, eliminating the negative." This was the way he lived.

These principles don't mean anything unless they are actually lived. Jesus did not just talk about these truths, Jesus *lived* them! Unless these truths are put into expression they don't mean anything. We need to consciously live by these laws and manifest them.

We can only have that which we think we are worth. The same is true with all the aspects of this principle. Once again, we can only have in our lives that which we are willing to be. If we want love then we need to, first of all, be loving. If we want forgiveness, then we need to be forgiving.

It is one thing to want physical strength, for example. However, if a person just sits and says, "I want strength," and never exercises, they are not going to have strength. So, just as we receive outer strength from exercising muscles, we receive inner strength from practicing the truth.

Remember those words of Jesus from the Lord's Prayer: "Forgive us our debts, as we also have forgiven our debtors." Our debts are forgiven as we have been willing to forgive another's. The only thing that can happen for us is *that which we provide the space for.*

It is up to us to open the way, and in opening up that way we find that interesting connections begin to appear in our lives. These connections will be further discussed in the chapter on serendipity. For now, we open up the way by becoming as children, finding that these principles do work, as they always have and as they always will.

2

The Spiritual Law of Love

Part One

*I sought Thee at a distance, and did not know
that Thou wast near. I sought Thee abroad,
and behold, Thou wast within me.*
St. Augustine

*I believe that the reason of life is for each
of us simply to grow in love.*
Tolstoy

Spiritual laws are not truly separate laws, for they are all interconnected rather than independent of one another. Spiritual laws are all sub-sets of the One Law: *there is only one presence and one power in this universe, which is God, which is good, and which is omnipotent.* But for purposes of clarification and of understanding more about how these principles work, the One Law has been broken down and its various aspects referred to as separate "laws."

This chapter is about the Spiritual Law of Love, which can also be seen as the law of attraction, and of acceptance. The Law of Love and the Law of Consciousness are very close. We cannot withdraw the Law of Consciousness and expect the Law of Love to work, or visa versa. They work as units, together.

When we think of love, we usually think of only the romantic aspects of love. However, the romantic aspects of love exist because there is a *principle of love* that is working behind and through *all* forms of love, including romantic love. But the romantic aspects of love are only a fraction of the quality which is Love.

Eskimos have over forty words for *snow*. They have a word for snow that is grainy and a word for snow that is wet. There are specific words for large flakes and for blowing snow, and for every type of snow imaginable. I suppose if you lived with snow most of the year, and if snow was a major part of your life, you would also have dozens of words for snow.

Just as the Eskimos have a variety of words to describe different types of snow, the ancient Greeks had multiple words for specific aspects of love. They recognized *philos* or *philia*, which means brotherly love. This is the love we feel for one another. They spoke of *eros*, which means passion. Eros is often thought of in terms of romantic love, but passion by the Greeks meant more than simply passion between two people. Their understanding of passion also included passion for life itself.

The Greeks defined yet another aspect of love. This third aspect they called *agape*. Agape means *divine love*. From agape, all the other aspects and manifestations of love pour forth. Agape is that which draws the best out of us and the best out of every situation that we are in. This divine love is that which attracts and that which accepts, *unconditionally.*

When we love one another, we accept one another. Unconditional love means that we accept another being for who and what they are, without any fear of what they might be, and without any need to change what they are. Unconditional love is *real* love. Unconditional love is acceptance.

We've all heard that "love is a magnet." This saying refers to the attractive power of love. Love draws out of every situation the *best.* Being a universal principle, love works through us as a magnet does. Love draws, rather than forces. We may sometimes think that the real power of this universe is within the people and institutions that are *forcing,* attempting to subject their will upon us. But the true power of this universe is that still voice within us. That still, soft voice draws the best out of us, and draws the best out of every situation.

We really have two inner voices. One voice tends to be very still, while the other shouts at us. The voice that shouts is the voice of moral authority. That is the old voice of the conscience, and that voice tells us all that we have learned and had passed onto us, true or not. The shouting voice comes from our parents, grandparents, great-grandparents, and so on, telling us all about life. The shouting voice is full of moral judgments. Sometimes the shouting voice, the conscience, can be a helpful guide, yet oftentimes it is very limiting.

We also have within us another voice, an intuitive presence which is the voice of Spirit, the voice of God. This voice does not force us, this voice never tells us "do not." This is a *leading* voice, always drawing us out of our small self and into our true state of being. The voice of Spirit always has us see possibilities where there weren't any possibilities. This voice allows us to feel better about ourselves and others.

This still voice draws out of us nothing less than the remarkable. We have not yet begun to realize what we have until we have listened to the still voice that speaks to each of us. That still voice, that *intuitive presence*, is the activity of love.

It says in the scriptures that God is love. God *is* love, and if we want to know more about God, we need to know more about love. We need to know more about how love exists, and more about how love expresses itself. And we need to know this not just through our intellect, but in our hearts and by our loving thoughts and actions. Instead of experiencing God as a being "out there," we can manifest God *here* by expressing love. We can experience God as the activity of love, and feel ourselves part of that love. *If we are to know God, we need to know love.*

Once again, love does not force, love draws. Love is drawing us to whatever our highest fulfillment is; love is drawing everything in this universe to its highest fulfillment.

Have you ever noticed that often we are at exactly the place where we most need to be, for ourselves as well as for others? We may see ourselves in a situation that unfolds the meaning of our presence there perfectly. A few years back, I was flying one leg of a trip, from Denver to Kansas City. There was a fellow sitting next to me, probably in his mid-forties. I picked up a magazine and started to read. This man, whom I'll call Ben, turned to me and said something to begin a conversation, and I responded. It was one little subject after another, until finally this whole flood of words and emotions came out of him.

Ben was the president of a high-tech firm in California, and was doing very well financially. He was flying back to his original home of Kansas City, which he had not seen in almost thirty years. Ben said that he had left as a young man, determined never to return again. His father had, he felt, so alienated him that Ben never wanted to go home and never wanted to face his father again.

Now it appeared that Ben's father was dying, so Ben had caught this flight at the last moment. His father was going in for surgery the next morning. But because the doctors expressed little hope that his father was going to survive the operation, it was important for Ben to get to the hospital that night to talk to his father. Ben did not know what he was going to say, and he was scared on that plane flight, almost to the point of being in tears.

Ben told me that he didn't think he could tell his father what he was feeling. He explained that in his youth his father had rejected him and cut him off, rarely allowing him to finish a sentence. Ben asked me, "What am I going to do? What am I going to say to him? 'Hi there, good to see ya'? And after that I just walk away and he dies? I have all these things built up in me, that I need to say."

I asked him, "What do you need to say?"

He took a deep breath and said, "I guess what I really need to say to my father is, 'Despite all the things that I never understood, I love you'."

I said, "Why can't you tell him that you love him?" Ben shook his head, "Because he'd just turn away and pretend I didn't say it." I told him that maybe his father *would* turn away, but I added, "evidently *you* need to say it."

After he continued talking about the situation for awhile, Ben did begin to express some hope. Even in this difficult situation, he began to feel that if he could express his deepest feelings, everything would work out right.

Several weeks later I received a letter from Ben. He wrote that he had told his father that he really loved him and that he had experienced such a warm and loving response from his father that he could hardly believe it. He said that the time recently spent with his father was one of the most wonderful times in his entire life.

The interesting thing was, Ben had gone to Kansas City feeling that his visit was going to be a time of last rites for his father. But his father went through the surgery beautifully, and was well on his way to recovery. "One of the aspects that's so wonderful about this," he wrote, "is that I'm going back to Kansas City now. I've got a family again." Thirty years had passed, and Ben had a family again.

How often we mistrust love! How often we're afraid of saying what we really feel. We fear that we're going to be rejected, so consequently we don't say what we need to. Then we find that life is not working. But life is not working *because we haven't allowed life to work*. We haven't followed that leading, that drawing in us, which is love.

We find that when we follow love, it works. Love not only draws the best out of us, but it draws the best out of every situation and every person. *There is an inherent power in all matter and thought, which is drawing everything to its highest fulfillment.* If we are acting in that presence of love, then we are going to draw the best out of ourselves, we are going to draw the best out of others, and we are going to find that events in our lives work out.

Ben demonstrated love working toward its highest good. What was necessary for his father's healing was not only the surgical operation undergone at the hospital, it was also, they felt, the surgery that Ben and his father performed on each other, by removing the old blocks that stood between them. This healing was done quite simply, with just a few words, *through the presence of love.*

The presence of love is truly a powerful force, and the life of Star Daily is a tremendous example of this power. Star Daily was a notorious criminal back in the 1930's. He was one of those people that no one believed could be rehabilitated. Star had been arrested so many times that he'd been put away as a habitual criminal. Because of this, the prison even tried to keep him separated from the other prisoners.

Somehow, Star came across some Unity literature. Although he had never been involved in Unity, the message affected him deeply. He read the pamphlets and suddenly realized that he had missed the whole point of life. He saw that he'd been rampaging angrily through life, thinking that everyone owed him something, instead of finding through love what he needed, and by being a part of life.

Star Daily began to practice love. He began to love his fellow inmates, and he began to love his jailers. He decided to try to do everything he could to make his life 180 degrees different than it had been. He was in prison with the understanding that he would never be released again, so Star decided to make his prison home a place where he could feel the presence of love.

Star so moved the entire prison that the warden himself supported Star's parole and eventually even a pardon. Star ended up writing a book titled <u>Love Opens Prison Doors</u>; it was a best-seller years and years ago, and sold for quite a long time. Star's message was this: by simply applying the presence of love in our lives, love would work to draw the best out of every situation and every individual.

We may or may not be in a physical prison, but we may feel like we are in a prison of problems and circumstances that are beyond our control, like Ben. He was certainly in a prison. If there was any place that Ben did *not* want to be, it was on that plane bound for Kansas City. But truly, love does open doors in our lives. Love draws the best out of everyone, and love draws the best out of situations that we encounter. Love unites us with our good, and when we follow the inner leading, we find that love works.

The problem is that often we doubt. We hesitate and we think, "What if love does *not* work?" I've asked myself that question many times. But, if love did not work, would it make any difference?

Blaise Pascal, the French philosopher and scientist, introduced what he called his "wager." There were people proclaiming that God did not exist, so Pascal basically asked, "What if God *does* exist? Would it not serve me better to act in my life as though God does exist?   And if God does *not* exist, would it diminish my life any?   Yet if God does exist, then would not my life be more united with that oneness?"   This is what is called Pascal's Wager.

When we take risks, when we are willing to express love, it may be the most difficult thing for us to express.   This is because we are not used to listening to that still voice within. The shouting voice has become an invisible controller in our lives.   By listening to the still voice, and by expressing love, we are breaking a deep, unconscious habit, and adding a new dimension to our lives.

Inherent in all matter and thought is a power which is drawing all existence to its *highest fulfillment.*   That is the Law of Love in you, which is the fulfilling of the presence of God.   The Law of Love brings the presence of God forth, into expression through our lives. John F. Kennedy used the quote, "God has no other hands and feet, save our own."

We are the hands and feet of God, and I would add, *the heart,* because love that is out there in the abstract is not love at all.   The abstraction of love can perhaps be diagramed or theorized, but that is its limit.   What is needed is the conscious, daily expression of love in our lives.

Love is the most real part of our nature. It is ironic that love is also probably the most difficult for us to reveal.   As we practice the Law of Love in our lives, we will find that love draws the best out of every situation.   If we want the situations in our lives to change, they can only truly change through the presence and the power of love, because love is the only presence and the only power.

3

The Spiritual Law of Love

Part Two

Love seeks no cause beyond itself and no fruit;
it is its own fruit, its own enjoyment.
St. Bernard

Paradise is always where love dwells.
Jean Paul Richter

Last chapter, we looked at some aspects of the Spiritual Law of Love and ways in which the law plays itself out in our lives. We saw that love draws the best out of everyone and every situation. We discussed the presence of love in that still voice within each of us. In this chapter, I want to focus on love as a transformative power, and show it at work in our lives.

Where is the best place to start in trying to understand love? The place to begin is with the *eternal presence of love*; the *divine* aspect. When we say that God is Love, and that the only power in this universe is God and that power is Love, what do we mean?

Look at the universe.   Scientists have discovered a new galaxy out there that is 4 billion light-years away, and the light from that galaxy has taken 4 billion years to arrive at the place where we can see it.   This means traveling for 4 billion years at 186,000 miles per second!   These scientists are actually able to see something that was happening right at the beginning of the creation of our universe.

What was the power behind that transformation of energy into matter that became our universe?   If we say that power is love, how exactly is it love and how does it work in our lives?

Mystics and poets throughout the ages have conveyed from the depths of their being that *God is Love.*   God is the creative presence and God is the energy which moves through the universe bringing all things together in right order.   God is the energy drawing the best out of every situation, drawing the best out of us, uniting us with what is really our good.   God is the presence working through all to create harmony and beauty.   That is what love in the fullest sense is doing.

In our lives, love is probably working in what seems to be an imperfect way because we are understanding love in a somewhat imperfect way.   We've seldom given love a chance to flow through ourselves completely, so we really don't know love on the intimate basis that we need to.   We need to learn to *trust* love; we need to let the presence of love nourish our hearts and minds.

Victor Frankl, in his book <u>Man's Search for Meaning</u>, writes about his experiences in some of the death camps during the Second World War. One recollection provides a stirring example of the nourishing power of love. During his last winter in the camps, on a morning when the temperature was well below freezing, the camp inmates were forced to start out on a march of twelve miles. Frankl said it was so cold that his feet had swollen and he had to wire his boots onto his feet. The inmates knew that if you were to fall down, you probably wouldn't get back up again.

Frankl wrote that as they were leaving the camp that morning, the person who was walking alongside of him turned to him and kind of smiled and said, "If our wives could only see us now!" He meant it in sort of a light way, and yet Frankl suddenly started thinking deeply about his wife. He thought about how much he loved her, and he thought about all of the wonderful things that they had shared together, and he started going over this and all that he loved in life. He didn't realize that his wife was already dead by that time, but he said it probably wouldn't have made any difference because the energy of that love was there so strong, it would have been there, just as strong, regardless.

Frankl relates that as he walked along, suddenly the 12 miles were over and he realized that he did not sustain any cold, and that he did not sustain any pain. He was not conscious of his body's suffering because he was focused on love: how much he loved his wife and how good it made him feel to think about her. He said he realized at that point how true it is when they say that love is the greatest power in the universe, that love can take us out of whatever depression or hurt or suffering we are in. When we start focusing on the love in our lives, any situation can be transformed.

In our lives we have situations where we don't know what to do. We all have them. There are situations that seem to have no sense to them. How do we treat these situations? The best way to treat them is *with love.* This is especially true in situations that are the most hurtful and the most painful; it is even more important to treat them with love.

In his book, <u>The Road Less Traveled</u>, Scott Peck examines love in a number of ways. He looks at romantic love, which he doesn't consider true love at all. The romantic is certainly an important aspect of love, but it isn't all of it; sometimes we focus only upon romantic love, and never get beyond that to the *sustaining aspects* of love.

Peck says that true love is our willingness to be loving even when we don't *feel* loving. It's our ability to be that which we don't feel at the moment; to still be able to express it. Peck also explains that true love is the effort to *extend ourselves.* True love is the effort to nurture another's spiritual growth, which at the same time nurtures our own.

An experience in a class a number of years ago made me realize just how important it is to treat situations with love. It also made me see how oftentimes we do other things *instead* of responding lovingly to experiences in our lives.

I was in the middle of teaching a class when a student jumped up and began shouting, "You're wrong! You don't know what you're talking about!" She was very angry and pointing at me, and I didn't know what to do. My initial reaction was to want to respond with, "Why don't you sit down? This is my class and if you want a class then go get your own!" This is often the kind of reaction we have, isn't it?

When people are hurting, they often lash out at others. What they are doing is advertising a deep need they have. They are advertising for love. Of course, we often see this as hostility being directed towards us, because advertising for love comes at desperate moments, when people are out of touch with their own loving energy. This need for love can manifest itself in unpredictable ways, and our task is to respond to those advertisements *with love*. No one is advertising for us to put them down, or for us just to pour our anger on top of their anger.

I did not realize it then, but now I understand that when people seem to be attacking us, they are not advertising for us to criticize them, and they are not advertising for us to insult or hurt them. They are really advertising for *love*.

Thankfully, in that classroom situation (and that's not the case in every situation in my life), I responded by taking a moment and letting her finish, and then coming back to her and saying, "Can I help you? I can tell you're hurting. Is there something I can do?" The woman was silent and then she began to cry. She opened up to the whole class, and everyone was right there, supporting her. Up until that moment, the class was absolutely tense.

I think we've all been in situations similar to this, where everyone wanted to escape a hostile or tense feeling that was going on. I didn't want to be there, either. And then suddenly the whole class was there, with her, in empathy. You could feel the love that was pouring out from each member of the class towards her. The woman went away feeling supported and loved and cared about, knowing that she had friends.

We transcended a situation that could have been a total disaster for everyone. I could have simply made her more angry and made her feel all the more alienated and all the more like there was no love in the universe. Instead, we all tried to support each other, *with love.*

Treating situations with love was the lesson that was remembered by everyone out of that whole series of classes more than anything else. How many times do we see people asking for love and we respond with something else? We often react defensively: by being angry, by being hurt, or by being resentful. But responding in this way only makes the situation worse for everyone.   If we can instead get in touch with that still presence within us, we can see people and situations more clearly, and so are able to bring in love and understanding.

When we treat situations with love, it is interesting that not only is that person getting the love, but we find that we *cannot give love away*. You can try to give love away, but the more you give away, the more love you have.

The more that you express love, the more love you create in your own life.   It's one of those things that actually is a multiplying process.   The more that we try to express love, the more love we have to express.   Love can not only transform but also create, *through us*.

Love doesn't exist when it is just love in the abstract.   Love exists because it is expressed.   How did the universe get created by love?   I don't know.   How did that power work to fling the stars all these billions and billions of miles?   I don't know.   But I do know that the basic cause behind the universe, and the basic cause behind each one of us, is love. And I know that if I'm not sure how a situation in my life needs to be handled, the answer is going to be *with love*.   Treating a situation with love means being open and willing to that other person.

When we learn verses from the Bible, we usually learn the 23rd Psalm, the Lord's Prayer, and the following section of First Corinthians, Chapter Thirteen.   Paul wrote:

> And though I bestow all my
> goods to feed the poor, and
> though I give my body to be
> burned, and have not love,
> it profiteth me nothing.
> Love suffereth long and is kind;
> love envieth not, love vaunteth
> not itself, is not puffed up,
> doth not behave unseemly,
> seeketh not her own, is not
> easily provoked, and thinketh
> no evil; rejoiceth not in
> iniquity but rejoices in truth,
> bareth all things, believeth
> all things, hopeth all things,
> and endureth all things. Love
> never faileth. Now abide in faith,
> hope, and love, these three, but
> the greatest of these is love.

Think about the *qualities* of love stated here. All the qualities of love are contained *within ourselves*. By meditating on these aspects of love, we can see how sharing these qualities can not only transform our own lives, but also the lives of others with whom we share love.

I looked in the dictionary for definitions of *love*, and there were 7 or 8 definitions given. Of these, almost every one of them included two words, *affection* and *attraction*. Love is our giving of affection, giving our understanding, and of placing ourselves in the other person's position.

Love is also attraction.   Love attracts from us all that we need to make our lives total and complete.   Love draws the best out of us.   Love draws the best out of every situation and out of every person.   *Love is the transforming power.* When we allow ourselves to be guided by love, it doesn't make any difference what is happening, the best is being drawn out of us.   The best is drawn out of the job we have, and the best is drawn out of any situation we are going through.   This is the way the universe works, drawing the best out *through love.*

Love is that which has drawn the best out of everything in the unfoldment of the celestial plan.   That is how love works.   It is not a power that forces itself upon anything, but rather, works in terms of harmonizing.

The true power of this universe never pushes upon you forcefully, but leads in a very warm and peaceful way.   Sometimes in a relentless way, too.   Love draws from us, pulling the best out from within us, allowing us to understand our real depth.

Once again, as Paul wrote, "Love never faileth.   Now abide in faith, hope, and love, these three, but the greatest of these is love."

4

The Spiritual Law
of Compensation

When you realize there is nothing lacking,
the whole world belongs to you.
Lao-tzu

There is a law that undergirds all of creation. It undergirds both the physical presence of creation and undergirds all of our thoughts. This is the Spiritual Law of Compensation. Emerson wrote about this law back in 1839, and we find that Jesus also mentioned it numerous times. Jesus taught, *"Give and it shall be given unto you. Good measure, shaken together, pressed down, and running over."*

In our lives, the Spiritual Law of Compensation is at work. Many people look at this law as a law of duality: there is right and wrong, there is black and white, there is good and evil.

But in truth, as we begin to look at this Law of Compensation, we discover that it is not a law of duality at all. Rather, it is a law of *balance*. The Spiritual Law of Compensation is a law that seeks to fill the void in life itself. So I call it either the Law of Compensation, using the term of Emerson, or the law of balance, or possibly even the law of the vacuum. It doesn't really make any difference what we call it. What *does* make a difference is living in loving harmony with the universe, for that is when we experience the *reality* of this divine principle.

We can use the example of the River Jordan in order to visualize this spiritual law. The River Jordan starts mainly on Mount Hermon, which is a mountain over 9,000 feet high on the Syrian-Lebanese-Israeli border. In fact, one branch of the river flows right out of Mount Hermon itself, coming from a cave. The river comes down into the Jordan Valley, through an area called the Hula Basin, and then descends into a large opening which we call the Sea of Galilee. At this point, the Jordan River is about 700 feet below sea level. The river finally winds down a very barren valley to the Dead Sea, which is 1,296 feet below sea level. The land there is the lowest on earth.

There are some very interesting things about this river that can help illustrate the principles of the Law of Compensation. The Sea of Galilee is really no more than a reservoir for the flow of the Jordan River. Around the Sea of Galilee there are beautiful orchards, with avocados, citrus fruits, and bananas growing in abundance. The Dead Sea is exactly what the name implies. The land is dead around it; there is nothing growing. The salts in the Dead Sea make up some 30% of the total of this sea, making it saltier than the Great Salt

Lake in Utah.

In our lives, we sometimes think that things are either given *from us* or received *to us*, and we look at our lives as a place that things sort of "bounce off." We may see ourselves either "giving something" or "receiving something," not realizing that we are much like the Jordan River. Where life is allowed to flow, giving and receiving, as in the Sea of Galilee, there is abundance and growth. But where there is *only* receiving, as in the Dead Sea, there is a vast expanse of barren lifelessness.

We are a channel for life if we allow life to flow through us, giving *and* receiving. The Law of Compensation is the law that reminds us that we are a part of this whole process of life. It reminds us that life does not happen "to us" or "from us." Life happens *through* us. Love happens through us, not to us. Joy happens through us, not to us. Prosperity happens through us, not to us.

If we embrace this spiritual law and apply it to our own lives, we will see that we are part of the flow and the energy of life. We will see that we are not bystanders, just standing back, watching life "happen." Life is moving through us. The Law of Compensation says that *as we give, life gives back to us.*

This law can also be compared to creating a vacuum. We need to create the space so that this principle can take over. We cannot have more illumination in our lives unless we're willing to give up the ignorance that we have. For example, we can't believe, at the same time, that the world is flat and that the world is round.

We need to give up one of those beliefs, because both of them cannot occupy the mind simultaneously. And if we've gone through life believing that the world is flat and everything about it is that way, that belief must be released before we can accept that the world is round.

In this same way, by giving up the limitations and the lack and the misunderstandings and the ignorance that we have, we are creating that vacuum. *We are creating the space for the positive in our lives.* Often, we need to let go of some old beliefs in order to be filled with illumination and create balance in our lives. But always, that balance is there, within each and every one of us.

Balance can come into expression in our lives when we give up old concepts and are willing to look at life in a new way. Interestingly, in our giving we create a greater capacity to receive. In our ability to give of understanding, we create a greater capacity for understanding. In our ability to give of love, we create a greater capacity for love in our lives.

As we give, not only do we receive, but we also have a greater capacity to receive, and thus a greater capacity to give. We make the channel greater in our own lives.

There is a rather well-known story about the man who wrote what was just a little book but which became a best-seller. It was not originally a book at all, but a speech, called "Acres of Diamonds," which was given over 5,000 times in America. It was one of the most famous speeches ever given, and its author's name was Russell Conwell.

Russell Conwell gave the speech for several purposes. The main idea behind it was simply that your good is where you are; that you start from where you are.

This idea is both very powerful and realistic. We don't start somewhere else, but we start right where we are. Our acres of diamonds are *right here* in whatever position or place or situation that we are experiencing *now*.

When Russell Conwell was a young man, he was a captain in the Union forces in the Civil War. He fought at the Battle of Shiloh, down along the southern Tennessee border. His unit was overrun by a Confederate force, and in the process of retreating across a burning bridge, Conwell dropped his sabre. His orderly, a fifteen-year-old boy named Johnny Ring, ran back to get it. In the hail of bullets and the fire on the bridge, the boy was killed.

When Conwell turned around and realized that this young boy, his orderly, had been killed while going back to retrieve the sword, he was so upset that he dismounted his horse and in the face of all the chaos, crossed back over the river to retrieve the young boy's body.

It is said that the fighting stopped, and there was a lull for that moment because everyone was taken aback by the Captain's action. Russell Conwell picked up the body of his young orderly, brought it back across the river, and as he was doing this he was thinking about how this boy had given his life for him. Russell stated that he said to himself at that time, "Johnny Ring is not dead, *but he lives*. And I'm going to make sure that he lives."

Russell dedicated himself at that point to something that I think all of us would find very difficult to do. He dedicated himself to living Johnny Ring's life: living eight hours a day for Johnny Ring, and eight hours a day as Russell Conwell. He fulfilled this in marvelous ways throughout his entire life. Whenever he gave the speech "Acres of Diamonds," he wasn't giving it as Russell Conwell, he was giving it as Johnny Ring. 5,000 times! In this way, he raised more than a million dollars, and this was over a hundred years ago. Conwell founded Temple University with the money earned from the speech given as Johnny Ring.

Russell Conwell, by also being Johnny Ring, lived a fuller life than he would ever have lived without that dedication. Russell increased his capacity to live, he doubled it. He was basically living two lives, fully and completely.

We have a tremendous capacity to give in our lives. We also have a tremendous capacity to receive. Unfortunately, sometimes we're *only* willing to give, and what happens is that we let the other doors within us be closed: doors that are being pounded upon to receive. Sometimes we're tremendous givers, but we're not very good receivers. And you know, the Jordan River wouldn't exist very long if it weren't for the snows and rains on the Lebanese mountains and on Mt. Hermon. It would dry up very soon.

We need *both* of these activities in our lives. If we think we're only here to give, we've only heard half of Jesus' statement "Give and *it shall be given unto you.*"

If we are only willing to give in our lives, we're going to find that soon we're going to run out. We have to understand that we are a *channel* for life, and that the Spiritual Law of Compensation is also a law of balance that is using us to keep the flow of life itself going. I want to share with you these words from Emerson:

Ever since I was a boy, I wished to write a discourse on compensation, for it seemed to me when very young, that on that subject life was ahead of theology, and the people knew more about it than the preacher's taught. The law holds with equal sureness for all right action. Love, and you shall be loved. All love is mathematically just, as much as two sides of an algebraic equation.

I have found that in my own life when I trusted this principle, it worked. I have found in my life that when I didn't think about this principle, but was actively practicing it, just how well it worked.

One time I had a car that was a perfectly fine car, but since I had two other cars, I gave one car away. Well, it was only a matter of weeks until two more cars were given to me. One of them was a car that I had given to my brother a couple of years earlier, and he ended up giving it back to me. I know why he gave it back, and if you've ever had an Austin Marina, you'll know why too!

It was very interesting how this happened. It had only been a couple of weeks and here I was with four cars instead of two. And right after my brother gave me the Austin, someone gave him a truck. He said, "Can you believe that? Just out of the clear blue, this friend who moved to Texas gave me his truck." I responded with, "Sure, it makes sense."

This all did make sense, because the Spiritual Law of Compensation *works*. We find that as we give, we do receive. We find that life is wonderful in its balance. Life never is out of balance.

The universe is never out of balance. Our lives might be out of balance, but the universe and life itself are never out of balance. When we are willing to give ourselves to life, life is most willing to give itself to us.

We often make some errors in under-standing this law. We think that the place we *give to* is the place that we will *receive from,* when this is seldom the case. Life keeps itself interesting for us. As we give, life does give back to us, but it gives to us in the most unexpected and incredible ways. Giving comes from channels that we had never imagined life would give through, and this is one of the joys of life.

We are open to this joy of giving and receiving when we allow ourselves to be channels for the flow of life. If we can move away from the idea that "I'm giving and I only have so much to give," and know that instead *we are a channel for life to give through us,* then we see that the Spiritual Law of Compensation is really that law of balance. We need to let go of the belief that there is lack in the universe in order to experience and recognize the loving balance of life.

If we can grasp that truth firmly, we can release the idea that somehow we are a limited entity that has only so much wisdom, only so much love, and only so much understanding. We can then release that concept of lack, and know that instead we are increasing our ability to give.

The people I have known that have truly been alive have been those individuals who were not afraid of life, and never thought that life was going to "run out" on them. They were willing to put themselves into life and enjoy life without the thought that somehow there wasn't enough life to go around. They knew that as we give of life, life gives itself back to us.

There is an illustration about life giving back to us in the Book of Malachi, the last book of the Old Testament.   God is talking about bringing the whole tithe to the storehouse. The Lord then says, "Prove me now herewith...if I will not open you the windows of Heaven and pour you out a blessing that there shall not be room enough to receive it." The idea is that if you give, you cannot "out-give" God. You cannot out-give that universal presence that is always seeking to give through us.

In Gerald Jampolski's book, <u>Love is Letting Go of Fear</u>, there's a statement which comes from *The Course in Miracles*. It says, "When you give, you only give to yourself."

We usually think that we're giving to *someone else*, and that we're giving something that *we own*. But life is a rather interesting thing. One spiritual teacher put it this way: "We never give of anything that we have. We only share it, because it's not ours to give. *All we can do is share that which God has given.*"

As we give, we open our ability to receive, so we really haven't given *away*. As we give, the greatest gift is to ourselves. If you want to feel that you truly are prosperous, you give. If you want to feel that you truly are strong, you give. If you want to feel that you truly are wise, you give.

The interesting thing is that wisdom, strength and prosperity flow back into your life through that channel.   "Give and it shall be given unto you.   Good measure, shaken together, pressed down and running over."

5

The Spiritual Law of Non-Resistance

Our doubts are traitors,
And make us lose the good we oft might
win
By fearing to attempt.
William Shakespeare

In the past four chapters we have been discussing various aspects of spiritual law. First there was the Law of Consciousness: that we can only *have* in our lives that which we're willing to *be*. Then we covered the Law of Love, which shows that the real energy of this universe is love. Love is never a power that is forcing itself upon us but rather is drawing out the very best from *within.*

Next came the Law of Compensation, which demonstrates that as we give we receive. We are making ourselves channels through which good can flow. It is not that we give *from ourselves* and the world somehow gives back this way, *to ourselves.* Rather, we're opening ourselves, more and more, to be that channel for life and for God's energy and illumination.

Now, the spiritual law that makes these other laws operative is the Law of Non-Resistance. As long as we are *resistant* we cannot be that channel, allowing love to work through us. Without our practice of non-resistance making all of these other spiritual laws operative in our lives, they are merely things that we read about and ideas we theorize. Non-Resistance is a *daily* practice.

Jesus probably put the Spiritual Law of Non-Resistance best when he said, *"Resist not evil, but overcome evil with good."* What many of us have been taught, probably ever since we were children, is to "resist evil," whatever we want to take this to mean. Here it is really *ignorance* that Jesus was speaking about, for evil acts only reveal ignorance of our true source, and *where we see evil is where our consciousness cannot see God.* This includes all the ignorance of the world, and all the ignorance that we, oftentimes, get ourselves involved in as well. We do not need to *resist* that ignorance. We do not need to fight it, and we do not need to allow our energy to be spent on ignorance. As Jesus reminds us, "*You* are the light of the world." So, we can move ahead, and focus our vision beyond ignorance.

It is easy to get stopped by a problem, and every one of us has been stopped by a problem many, many times in our lives. We focus on that problem, we fight with it, we work with it, and we think that the answer to the problem is in the problem itself. But the answer isn't located *in* the problem!

We do not find an answer in the problem, we find an answer by going *beyond* the problem. We find the answers by allowing our vision and creative energies to expand. Only when we move to that vision do we find the answers we seek.

So often, we get ourselves "stopped" in life and we wonder why nothing is working. This often has to do with the focus of our lives, which is on the problems, rather than upon the answers.

When we look at any aspect of life that *is* working, we find that there are creative people in those areas. Truly creative people are not focused upon the problems. They are focused on ways in which things *can* work.

When I think about people who focused on how things can work, one of my favorites is Frank Laubach. He was called the "modern day mystic." Laubach started the World Literacy Crusade. One motto he is known for is his "Each One Teach One" program. Now, there can be thousands of people commenting about the fact that we have an illiteracy problem in the world, and they can tell us all the statistics about the problem. Have you ever noticed how wonderfully we can innumerate statistics about problems? But no problem has ever been worked out just from the statistics about it. We have to go *beyond* the statistics of any problem.

Instead of just focusing on the problem, and the statistics surrounding it, Frank Laubach had the vision to look farther and say, "What can be done? What can *I* do?" As one person we normally don't think that we can do very much, but Laubach started a program where he taught a couple of people to read. These couple of people taught a couple more people, and what happened was a simple geometric progression.   Because of this program, in a matter of years there were a hundred million more literate people in the world.   A hundred million!   The simple act of one person starting out teaching two people rose from an idea that was not focused on the *problem*, but instead was directed towards an *answer*.

Non-resistance is really about our being focused on the answers of life, rather than on the problems.   *Not being resistant.*   Often we find that what we are most resistant to is our own good.

How are we resistant to our own good?   *If we allow ourselves to be led off our path, we are resistant to our own good.*   We are also resistant to our own good when we get too involved with our problems, and when we find ourselves worshiping the problems in life. Every one of us, I bet, has worshiped problems. Yet, by turning inward and listening to that still, small voice *within us*, we can move once again into the harmonious flow of life.

You   might   say,   "I   don't   worship problems!" But if we give a problem our full attention, if this is where our focus is, and if we continue giving the problem all of our worry and all of our concern and all of our energy, then we *are* worshiping it.   The problem has become, in a sense, our god.   So we become "out of the flow" and tend to feel frustrated and anxious. But when we quiet our minds, and let the dynamic, loving qualities of life shine forth, we find that we are facing our old problems in a new way. The problem is no longer a problem: a quantum leap has occurred and everything has changed, because we have become centered, and we have allowed ourselves to be loving in all situations.

What does it mean for us to be loving in all situations? There may be some situations in your life that seem quite difficult to even conceive of being loving toward. First, remember to love yourself. From the perspective of love, and by flowing peacefully through this loving universe, it would feel quite unnatural to approach a situation with anything except love. *Find the love that is living in yourself.* This is only possible by giving yourself the time to listen to that still, inner voice within, that is always working for your own good, and the good of the universe.

It may seem more convenient to listen to other people, or to do what is socially or culturally "correct." But when we act out of anxiety, haste, fear, or pressure from others, when we respond to action through anything except our true source, love, a situation can quickly escalate into what may become a chronic problem.

To approach a situation with love means to first give that divine love to yourself. Be alone, make a time and a space for that loving energy to be heard and felt. This is the first, most solid step to approaching all areas of life. Feel the love flowing through you, for you will experience a deep, resonant wellspring that will show you how *much* you are! You will see clearly that you are a miracle, and that all of life is a miracle, and you will find that by giving spiritual attention to all areas of your life, you are turning your daily existence into a meditation. Life then becomes a prayer, infused with gratitude and joy, and at the deepest level, peace.

Only when we stop focusing on the problems in our lives can we allow this peace to flow through us. A favorite story of mine has to do with a very successful businessman in New York. He was almost too successful in one way, because his success had also created a dissonance in his life. Because of all the events and tensions that were going on with his business, this man had tremendous stress. He was so caught up in his business problems that the stress level had built to the point where he found himself with a migraine headache that was just tearing him apart.

The migraine had been going on for three weeks when he finally went to his doctor. He told the doctor about his migraine, and he told the doctor about all the pressures that were occurring in his life. The doctor sat and listened to everything he had to say about all the stresses in his work, and how he was unable to deal with them.

Finally, the doctor wrote out a prescription and handed it to the businessman, who read it and exclaimed, "You've got to be kidding!"   The doctor told him, "No, I'm not kidding, I want you to do exactly what it says on that piece of paper."   But the man said, "You don't really mean for me to go out and do this?" The doctor firmly replied, "You'll know I'm not kidding when you get my bill!"

The piece of paper that the doctor wrote out said simply, "Go to Grand Central Station. Find someone there in need and help them." The businessman said, "I've got all these things to do.   How am I going to find the time to go to Grand Central Station and find someone in need and help them?"   The doctor replied, "I don't know, but that's what I'm prescribing you to do."

Well, the man did follow the prescription, and a wonderful lesson took place.   This businessman helped a small-town woman who was confused and lost, visiting New York for the very first time.   He was able to reunite her with her daughter, easily clearing up a frightening experience for a stranger to the intimidating city.   By thinking of another person and of their problems, and by immersing himself in trying to help them, this suffering man was able to get away from the stresses and problems of his own existence for a little while.   His migraine of three weeks vanished into thin air when he put the doctor's orders into action.

In his poem "I Am There," James Dillet Freeman writes that we can know God only when we get *ourselves* out of the way.

Getting ourselves out of the way is sometimes a very difficult thing to do. It is difficult because we have been convinced that the energies that we use to create a problem are somehow the same energies that we need to use to overcome it, and that's not true. We need to focus beyond the problems, by *allowing ourselves to get out of the way.*

We are often afraid to get ourselves out of the way, because we think that if we do get ourselves out of the way, then we aren't going to *be* anybody. We think, "If I really got myself out of the way, what would I be? I wouldn't be needed." And that's not true, either.

Sometimes we think that if we get ourselves out of the way, our personality will somehow be less. But the people who truly get themselves out of the way are not individuals with less personality, they're the ones with the richest personalities! They are the ones who are humble, caring, magnetic, and dynamic; they are people who have a sense of peace.

There's an old Unity affirmation that goes way back, and while it is very simple, it is a meaningful statement of non-resistance: *I let go, and I let God.* This doesn't mean that we let go in the way we sometimes think we let go.

Letting go does not mean that we ignore a problem. Letting go and letting God is an *action* statement, just as we need to understand that non-resistance is an action law. Non-resistance does not mean that nothing is done. Rather, it means that our energies are focusing in a new direction.

Letting go and letting God means we let go of all the things that have been *blocking* the creative energies in our lives. We let go of the problems, and we let go of the worry and frustration. We walk away from the problem part and we begin to focus in on the answer. We begin to focus on what *does* work in our lives. We focus in on our imaginative properties and energies, and we let them flow, and we move with them. We let go of worry, doubt, fear, and anxiety. We let go of all the feelings of failure and the feelings of lack that we have.

The word *worry* itself has telling roots. It comes from an old Anglo-Saxon word, and it originally meant "to strangle." If you've ever thought about how worry affects us in our lives, you know that it certainly does strangle us. *Worry cuts off our healing and creative energies.* Anxiety strangles us also, as do doubt and fear. All that focusing on the problem does is cut off our energies. We need to go beyond that.

When we are focusing on a problem, our resistance is very much present. When we become non-resistant, we get ourselves into the place where we allow the creative energy of the universe to flow through us. When we become non-resistant, we're one with that creative energy. Then we're no longer part of the problem, but part of the answer.

Another statement of non-resistance that Jesus made was, "Blessed are the meek, for they shall inherit the earth." The word *meek* originally meant *those who are teachable, those who are open.* Meek was referring to people who were approaching life from another dimension, who had another way of looking at reality. Jesus was talking about those who are willing to put aside the way that they have approached life in the past and to look at life in a completely new way.

When we become trapped by seeing situations through a "short focus" lens, we become the prisoners of our own narrow and rigid reactions, habits, and beliefs, so that we are no longer *meek.* But when we move away from our strictly small self focus, we find ourselves increasingly open, discovering moment by moment just how exquisite this universe truly is.

James Thurber was a terrific writer and cartoonist who used a good deal of humor when reflecting on certain situations in his life. He once wrote about an experience he had gone through in college. In biology class, James was supposed to look at a slide through a microscope and then draw what was on the slide. Whenever he looked in the microscope, he saw a circle with an oval in the middle, which was what he drew every time.

His biology instructor was frustrated with James, and James was just plain frustrated. His teacher finally said, "If you don't draw what's on the slides, I'll fail you." So James failed. Years later, he figured out why he couldn't see anything on those slides in his biology class. He had been *focusing so short* that he had been looking at the reflection of his own eye!

Isn't this what we oftentimes do? When we're looking at a problem, we may be focusing so short that all we're doing is seeing the problem back again, and that's all we can see. *We need to focus beyond the problem, so that we can see the potential and the answers.* Any of you experienced with photography know this truth from focusing a lens.

If you wish to photograph a mountain range, but there is a cyclone fence between you and the lovely peaks, it is quite simple to just focus the wires of the fence out of view. Any child who has fooled around looking through screen doors has come across the same phenomenon, so a photographic lens is only mimicking a quality of nature, the functioning of our own eyes. When we move away from our small self focus on the problems, our vision expands, and we begin to be receptive to the answers.

Again, we need to look at our lives and to know that we are open to new directions, and that we are not, as Jesus said, *resisting evil.* Instead, we are overcoming evil with good by adding new energy and new creative dimensions into our own lives. We are then able to experience life in a completely different way.

Every one of us has probably been involved in a situation where we have been resistant about something, possibly a particular person. We can see that one type of resistance is holding anger and being non-forgiving of another.   So being non-resistant is really also about being forgiving.

Non-resistance is an action law. *Being non-resistant is allowing ourselves to listen to God.* Remember to listen to that still voice rather than paying attention to all the endless lists of things people tell us. It is truly amazing how much energy and focus we can give to situations that are far off-center, when we could be meditating and listening to the voice of Spirit within.

When you give yourself the time and space to listen to your still, inner voice, others may not understand. You may have a busy life, and so feel that you can't spare the time to be still. *It is up to you*, for this is the door that opens forth the imprisoned splendor, the door within, that leads to your true self. *You are the keeper of the key.*

Let go and let God. Let go of the anxiety and the worry, and let your focus be on all the good that is in your life.   When you start focusing on the good, you'll find an opening out into new ways. "Resist not evil, but overcome evil with good." It works.

6

The Spiritual Law of Being

These inner riches do not depend upon outer conditions, and we must not bind ourselves by believing that they do.
Myrtle Fillmore

The last five chapters have been about some of the separate aspects of the *one principle* of the universe. Chapter One was the Law of Consciousness, which states that we can only *have* that which we are willing to *be*. For example, we can only have forgiveness if we are willing to be forgiving.

Next we concentrated on the Law of Love, which reveals that everything in the universe works from center to circumference. It shows that all of the energies of this universe are attracting energies. These energies are drawing out from us the highest and the very best that is within ourselves.

This was followed by the Law of Compensation, which reminds us that things do not come "to us" and "from us" but rather that things flow *through us*. We are a part of the channel of God's energy and God's substance and God's love, and this universe is in balance.

Last chapter, we focused on the law that puts all of the others into motion, the Law of Non-Resistance. The Law of Non-Resistance works when we get ourselves out of the way and when we focus *beyond* our problems. By letting go of and freeing ourselves from all the barriers and walls that we have built, we can truly appreciate our lives, knowing that the energy and wisdom of God is within every single one of us.

Now we will explore the Great Law, the Great Principle, which is the Spiritual Law of Being, the one spiritual principle out of which all the others unfold. The Law of Being is phrased concisely in this basic statement of Unity's teaching, "There is only one presence and one power in the universe, God, the good, omnipotent."

There is only one presence and one power in the universe. Most of us, however, have operated under a very different premise for a good part of our lives. We may have thought that the universe was acting against itself, and that there were two powers, one good and one evil. We may have also been taught that there was Hell and the devil.

What we have when we accept these beliefs is a very confused universe. It is not surprising that we would have confused individuals. Given this outlook, it is no wonder that we could go through life sometimes trusting life to uphold us and support us, and at other times feeling that life has just pulled the rug out from under us. Because we saw such a duality in this world, we never were sure about what was operative in our lives and what was not.

However, every individual and every circumstance is working toward a higher potential in their own unique way. There may be beliefs of some individuals or organizations that we may not agree with. Remember to continue to be humble, in Jesus's words, to be *meek*, and to know that everyone we meet has a special lesson for us. We ourselves have all gone through transitions in the ways in which we have thought and acted. It is very easy to get excited and to feel joy at experiencing life in a new way, yet we cannot forget to practice compassion and acceptance for all those we meet. The splendor within us is truly splendid and looks upon everyone with love, guiding us wisely through every situation in our lives.

It is not easy for many of us to conceive of this universe as being *absolute good*. We can say a song is good, we can say that ice cream is good, we can say that's a good movie, and those are all relative terms. Something, however, exists behind these relative terms: the functioning principle of absolute good, that divine presence which is the fabric of the universe. The word "universe" does not just refer to the physical world that we see, but also that which is unseen. There are dimensions we know and dimensions we don't know. All of them are aspects of absolute goodness.

The Law of Being refers not only to the transcendent quality of good. It also refers to the immanent aspect of good which is individually focused in every one of us, just as it is focused in every part of this universe. We can say that God, or goodness, *is holographically projected within all creation.*

A scientist I knew once showed me a hologram. It consisted of a clear plastic plate and a small laser. The laser was focused so that its beam would project at an angle through the plate. Behind the plate could be seen an image of a watch stand, and on it was a pocket watch. The image consisted of another stand also, and hooked into this stand was a magnifying glass.

Looking through the clear plate, I could see both of these items. When I changed my viewing angle and looked through the hologram of the magnifying glass, I could see the watch through it, magnified! It was even more disorienting to realize that I was watching a magnifying glass that *was not there* magnifying a watch that *was not there.*

The scientist asked me, "If I were to take this plate and smash it, and just take a fragment from it, and I passed the laser through that shard, what would we see?" I replied, "Well, we'd probably see a part of the watch or a part of the stand or a part of the magnifying glass." He said, "No, if you passed the laser through even just a broken piece of this plastic, you would still see the *whole* watch and the *whole* magnifying glass, each on their respective stands. Everything. Any piece that you can pick up, no matter how large or how small, will be able to project the *entire image*."

All of the principles of God are in every aspect of the universe. That is not only the universe that we see out in the physical world. It applies to the universe *within us* as well.

Within each and every one of us are all of the ideas and all of the intelligence of the universe. There is not an idea that has ever gone into this universe, or ever will go into this universe, that is not already within us. This doesn't mean that we are always expressing it very well, but it's there. It is a part of our nature, a part of our being. It cannot be otherwise. One poet put it this way, *"God is nearer than breathing, and closer than hands and feet."*

When we look at the example of the holographic plate, we see that the complete hologram was contained in each of its separate fragments. In this same way, God can be seen as being holographically located in all of creation. That *Christ presence* can be seen as manifest inside every one of us. In every aspect of your being is God. In every aspect of every situation that you go through, there is that never-failing presence of goodness.

We can even see goodness where we least expect it. In this regard, the story of Velcro is an amusing illustration. A scientist/inventor went to church with his wife one Sunday, and he found himself sitting through one of the most boring services imaginable. It was so boring that he began looking around for something to distract himself. Soon, he was counting the holes on the ceiling tiles. Next, he saw a little burr that was caught on his pants, and he began to examine it. As the sermon droned on, he was pulling the burr off his pant leg and putting it back on, over and over again. He began deeply wondering why that little burr kept sticking to his pants.

After church the inventor took the burr home with him, and put it under a magnifying glass. He saw dozens of tiny hooks on the ends of the spines of the burr, and thought, "Can I duplicate these hooks and create something useful out of it?" So you see, even from a bad sermon came something good, Velcro! I've even asked myself on certain Sundays when I didn't feel like I was coming across quite like I wanted to, "I wonder what they're inventing out there?" You never know, do you?

Albert Einstein liked the quote from Ralph Waldo Emerson, "God doesn't play with dice." The understanding expressed in this saying is that the universe is *orderly*. Life itself is orderly. At the deepest level, we don't have a life or a universe where some parts are warring against other parts. In this universe, certain truths are always operative and in harmony.

Another statement of Einstein's was, "The universe is friendly." This seems a rather odd quote. It can even appear flippant, especially if we are currently going through a difficult time.

But Einstein was not a naive or cavalier thinker, and *he lived through some particularly sobering times*. When we think of the immense suffering Einstein witnessed, it seems more rational to say the universe is neutral, or even cruel. Yet Einstein, a remarkably wise man, stated that the universe is *friendly*. What could this possibly mean?

As a deep, broad, and meditative individual, Albert Einstein was perceiving the universe from a heightened state of awareness. He was looking at existence as an astronaut looks back upon the earth, and experiencing the infinite joy of creation. His insight transcended the veil of appearances and peered into a richer truth. He journeyed inward. A true understanding of "the universe is friendly" is not purely intellectual, limited to solely mental processes. It is wisdom from the very center of your being, who you *really* are.

When we allow our small selves to get out of the way, and we focus beyond our limits and problems, we are then open to experiencing this "cosmic friendliness." This liberating and transformative realization is expressed so clearly in India's Taittiriya Upanishad:

> *From joy all beings have come,*
> *by joy they all live,*
> *and unto joy they all return.*

The joy and friendliness of the universe is there, always, at our very center. It is relief from suffering even when circumstances would call for sorrow and misery. It is an energy so eternal, so vast and so indescribable in its *allness* that absolutely nothing can lessen that energy. That is how powerful the splendor, now imprisoned, truly is.

Often there are rigid beliefs we cling to tightly that are actually holding back our spiritual growth and limiting our receptivity to this cosmic joy. For some, a deep-seated belief in an entity such as "the devil" can be a tough one to give up, because it is so easy to say, "The devil made me do it!" How much easier can we have it than that? We have then been able to delegate all responsibility in our lives to something else, in this case a being who tempts us off our path, and whom we use as a scapegoat. I think if I were the devil, I'd be pretty angry! There can be no real growth while allowing something else to negate our own responsibility for ourselves.

Another old belief that can be hard to let go of is the belief in Heaven and Hell. It is interesting that in the Bible, Hell was a place called *Ga Hinnom*, or the Hinnom Valley. The Hinnom Valley borders the southern edge of the old city of Jerusalem. This was the place where all the garbage of the city was brought, through a gate called the "dung gate." The dung gate is still in existence today. All the refuse was thrown into this valley, and fires were burning there constantly.

Although the Hinnom Valley was a place that people did not especially want to visit, they knew it was essential. Hell, a fiery garbage dump, is most accurately seen as a necessary process of purification, not a place of eternal punishment where "sinners" end up when they die. *Hell is located within ourselves.*

Hell is what we go through in the process of removing all the blocks inside ourselves as we open to the good in our lives. Hell is a tormented state of existence with terrific potential for spiritual growth. It is here, in the most confusing, brutal moments of our lives that we are *really* tested for our mettle. Hell is to be respected. We may choose to draw from the wisdom gained through torment, or we can choose to deny our hell and wait until the same inferno blows through our lives again. This universe is endlessly patient, and unresolved hells will always return, until worked through completely and our lessons fully learned.

Hell is a part of our own nature, which we all experience, just as Heaven is. The poet Whittier summed it up nicely when he wrote:

> The stern behest of duty,
> the doom book open thrown,
> the Heaven you seek,
> the Hell you fear,
> *are with yourselves alone.*

Every one of us has gone through times of purification that we would rather not have gone through. We have understood that Hell was there, and that we have passed through it. We've understood that we are probably better off for it, but we'd just as soon not have known about it. We have felt isolated and not connected with the flow of the universe. We've experienced Hell.

Every one of us has experienced Heaven as well. Heaven is that state of consciousness where we truly are one with the universe. This is when we experience ourselves as one with the loving qualities of the universe, when we are one with all the truths that we know, and when we are letting the true source work in our lives. There can be no Heaven or Hell that could possibly be created *out there* that isn't somehow more poignantly known within ourselves. Heaven and Hell are within *ourselves*.

It is so easy to get tied up in false beliefs about the universe and about ourselves, not realizing that the ultimate truth of our being is goodness, absolute goodness. Some of the followers of Jesus once began to call him "good." But he corrected them by saying, "Why do you call *me* good? There is but One that is good." Jesus was focusing on the same principle.

I *as an individual* may or may not do things that are good, and may or may not do things that are intelligent, but within me and within everyone is all the intelligence and goodness of the universe. Jesus said, "The works that I do, you shall do also, and greater works than these shall you do." Once again, he was trying to make us aware of that essence of life and that essence of goodness within every one of us. In order to get in touch with that absolute goodness, we have to let go of all the roadblocks, barriers, limitations and preconceived ideas that we have built up. Then we can experience that essence of goodness which is the true nature of our being.

We are in a universe that works. We are in a universe where all the aspects of good are linked, one with another. So often time is wasted in our lives, worrying about things that *might* happen and fretting about the future. I think of how often people get so involved in wondering what it is going to be like for them to exist in Heaven one day, when they are living in Hell right now. You cannot experience Heaven at another point in time *if you can't understand it right here.*

Life is indeed eternal, but we need to focus on the *Now*. This truth also applies to our understanding of Hell. Some might think, "Well, it's going to be all right because so-and-so is going to Hell." We've probably heard people say that of others. However, this negates the true essence of life. It is not that I don't believe in the eternal quality of life, because I do. In every way I believe in it, and I also believe there is a continuum which is beautiful and ever-fulfilling and ever-unfolding. However, we need to be focused on the time in eternity that all of us can truly know and believe in, which is *Now*. Heaven at some future time, or Hell at some future time, or anything at some future time, means nothing.

God is good, and all that can follow this moment, if we are willing to accept it, is good. That goodness is far beyond what our eyes have been able to see, our ears have been able to hear, our hearts have been able to feel, and our minds have been able to comprehend.   That goodness is absolute.   It is able to be formed in any way that minds are capable of envisioning it, and to the same degree that we can accept it.

The truth of our being is that all of the love and wisdom of the universe is *already within us*.   As a part of the creative process of the universe, it is up to us to unfold that wisdom, to express it, to live it and to be it.

This universe is not set up to create us to fail, because the universe is both orderly and friendly.   It seeks the highest and the best for each of us.   *There is but one presence and one power in this universe, and in ourselves.*   That presence and that power is holographically located, is good, is omnipotent, omniscient and omnipresent.   What an extraordinary difference this realization can make in all of our lives.

7

Serendipity

*All things so interwoven are
that thou canst touch the flower
without troubling the furthest star.*
Francis Thompson

𝕾erendip was a country that existed long ago, in a place later to be known as Ceylon. We now call this exotic island Sri Lanka.

According to legend (whose only known surviving text is an Italian compilation of stories and novellas), there were once three princes from Serendip, and they had many unusual adventures. The princes were alert and wise, and they sometimes came across marvelous and unexpected discoveries while in pursuit of something else.

The Italian printing of these tales is called the *Peregrinaggio*. Published in 1557, the *Peregrinaggio* is relatively recent, for the tales are ancient and have deep roots in the oral tradition throughout the orient. Newer still is the word *serendipity*, which was borne by an Englishman of letters (among many other interests), Horace Walpole.

As a child, Horace had read the rare *Peregrinaggio*. He loved the stories, for they were exciting and from a far away land, with these majestic, colorful princes who were always coming upon wild situations. When he grew up, Horace thought about those tales, but no one could tell him anything about them. Finally, after many years, through a strange accident that was itself serendipitous, Walpole found these curious tales again, and was eventually drawn to create the word *serendipity*. But what does serendipity mean?

Webster's Third Edition reads: "the gift of finding valuable or agreeable things not sought for-- a word coined by Horace Walpole, in allusion to a tale, *The Three Princes of Serendip*, who in their travels were always discovering, by chance or sagacity, things they did not seek." But Walpole himself defined the word differently, using *and* in place of *or*, for sagacity and chance are both vital for serendipity. *Sagacity* refers to our own sense of awareness, or keenness of discernment. The princes of Serendip displayed their sagacity through wisdom, intuition, and alertness.

Serendipity occurs when there is the flowing mixture of the *chance* of the external, and the *awareness* of the internal, meeting in a playful dance. It is never sought, and always brings great joy.

Mysterious as it is, serendipity follows certain principles. It is always unexpected, and its delightful presence shows the surprising aspect of divine love. The recipient who experiences this caring gesture strongly feels what is always there, *the friendliness of the universe.*

Many of us may think that serendipity is a happy chance, and that it is, but we need to have a keenness of sense about us in order to even see the happy chance. If we are dulled, or our view is constricted and narrow, how can we possibly expect to find something wonderful, or even recognize a true gift when it is delivered to us?

We can recognize our gifts when we recognize and love our true selves. If our awareness is alert, and our mind is letting love flow through it, and we are respectful of our intuition and our wisdom, then our lives become like the three princes of Serendip. Unexpected joys are always popping up in the most unexplainable places, and we in turn are spreading even more love into situations that may not have expected that gift from us. When we live a life of serendipity, we are led to deep and clear insights about the whole, rich cosmos that we are part of.

The Bible contains several very clearly serendipitous types of events. The story of Joseph in the book of Genesis is one such example. Joseph's own brothers sold him into captivity in Egypt. He ended up in the household of Potiphar, first as a slave but eventually as the headservant of the house-hold. Potiphar's wife then developed an interest in Joseph. Joseph realized that this was wrong, and did not return her affections. Potiphar's wife became angry and told lies about Joseph to her husband, so Joseph was thrown in jail.

While in jail, awaiting probable execution, Joseph came to know two of the Pharaoh's servants, who were also behind bars. One of them was the chief baker and the other the chief cupbearer. During this time, Joseph interpreted dreams for the prisoners, and his insight gained him respect among them.

The cupbearer was eventually released from the prison and returned to his post, but Joseph continued to live within its confines. One night, the Pharaoh had a strange dream. He dreamt of seven fat cattle and then of seven lean cattle. This dream affected him profoundly, but he did not know what its message was. When the cupbearer heard of this, he told the Pharaoh about Joseph, and how Joseph had a gift for deciphering dreams.

Joseph was able to interpret the Pharaoh's dream. He said that the fat cattle represented seven years of feasting and that the lean cattle indicated a seven year famine. The Pharaoh took Joseph's words seriously, and positioned Joseph as the second-in-charge of all Egypt. In his powerful office, Joseph developed a massive program for storing grain, in case a famine should come to pass.

When a famine did arrive, people flooded into Egypt from all of the surrounding areas, trying to find food. Lo and behold, a group came from the highlands of Judaea seeking food, and it included Joseph's brothers. Joseph played a trick on them at first, but later accepted his brothers into Egypt to share the stored grain. Joseph said, "You might have

meant it for evil, but God meant it for good."
One translation of the Bible even says, *"You did
not know, but God did."* This is the meaning of
serendipity, that God *does* weave a pattern, but
only when we get ourselves out of the way are
we able to see it.

Joseph's captivity, and even his imprison-
ment, turned out to be serendipitous. His
character and resolve were strengthened, and
by his action and foresight, untold suffering
was able to be averted. These kinds of
serendipitous events happen all the time. They
really are the way that life can work.

Often we may find life full of not serendipity, but difficulty. We are tuned into a
variety of difficulties. Are you or is someone
you know crisis-prone? Are you or this person
always living on the edge of crisis, to the point
where you think, "This is the way life works?"

When we start thinking about the
meaning of "works" and "crisis", we realize they
are opposites. Crisis is not how life works; it is
how *we* operate when we get our small selves
in the way of life's flow. It is not only external
events that bring crisis into our lives, it is our
reaction to external events. When we live by
the serendipitous thread of life, things start to
work together, and we stop being tossed about
by continual crisis. In Jesus' words, "All things
work together for good for them that love the
Lord."

Serendipitous events are happening all
the time, but we often are not aware of them

and so do not notice. All of the forces of the universe are always working for you. But when the small self is overly consumed with its problems, this can be nearly impossible to see.

The following stories describe some serendipitous events in the lives of historic persons. These dramatic and surprising twists of the universe are all part of the play of serendipity.

Back in 1776, John Adams, a representative from Massachusetts, took aside a young redhead from Virginia, whose name was Thomas Jefferson. Adams said to him, "I'd like to have you write a Declaration of Independence...independence from the crown of Britain." Jefferson was taken aback and responded, "Why don't you write it?"

Adams replied, "If I wrote the Ten Commandments, the Continental Congress wouldn't listen to them. You see, they look at me as a rabble-rouser. But if *you* wrote it, I know it would be listened to."

Jefferson had been a fairly shy member of the Continental Congress. He had spoken up very little, and he was a young, inexperienced politician. Yet he agreed to take on the job.

These two individuals were very different in several highly noticeable ways. They were not even affiliated with the same political parties. One was experienced, the other was not. Jefferson was from Virginia while Adams was   from Massachusetts, and these two colonies were poles apart at that time in history.

Yet   when   Jefferson   brought   the completed manuscript to Adams, a bond flowed between them.   Jefferson said that it felt as though the document wrote itself.   Some of the passages truly did seem scriptural: "We hold these truths to be self-evident, that all men are created equal, that they are endowed with certain inalienable rights, among these, life, liberty, and the pursuit of happiness."   Adams was elated.   He said, "If we could see this country fifty years down the road, we would see it growing out of its infancy and into maturity."

Both Adams and Jefferson wanted to return to their homes after they served in the Continental Congress, but they were called to ambassadorships   and   other   government positions.   Adams   became   the   second president.   Jefferson was his vice-president and eventually became president himself.   They both gave up a good deal of their lives for an ideal.

July 4th, 1826, found Jefferson very weak.   He asked what day it was.   He was told, "It is July Fourth."   Jefferson said, "Liberty forever."   Then he added, "Adams lives," and later that evening passed on.

Adams had been ill for some time.   He also asked what day it was on July 4th, 1826. He was almost ninety years of age.   He gave a final rally after being told that it was July

Fourth and said, "Liberty forever.   Jefferson lives." Then he, too, quietly passed on.

Two presidents died on the same day, July 4th, 1826. They were the individuals who were most responsible for the Declaration of Independence.   One was the instigator, the other the author. They both gave tremendous service to their country. And they both died on the 50th anniversary of the signing of the most important document of those colonies, even speaking the same dying words.

Is this only coincidence?   I don't believe so.   If we were to calculate the chances of two presidents dying on the same day, and that day being a significant part of both of their lives, the odds would be astronomical.   Time after time we see these stories of serendipity, these wondrous   events   that   defy   ordinary explanation.

Another story of serendipity revolves around Edwin Booth.   Edwin Booth was America's greatest Shakespearean actor of his day, possibly the best of his century. But on a fatal day in April, 1865, John Wilkes Booth, Edwin's brother, shot and killed Abraham Lincoln in the Ford Theater.

When Lincoln was assassinated, Edwin felt that his own life was over as well. He could never again, he felt, go back on the stage. He and his family were both disgraced and devastated by the murder committed by John Wilkes.

A few years later, Edwin was at a crowded train station. Suddenly, a young boy got shoved off the platform and onto the tracks, right in front of an oncoming train. Edwin quickly jumped onto the tracks, swiftly lifted the boy back onto the platform, and was himself pulled up by someone. It was not until some time later that Edwin found out that the boy he saved was Abraham Lincoln's son.

When Edwin received a letter from Mary Lincoln, he wept. He said, "This was obviously the grace of God, for nothing else could have freed me and allowed me to continue with my life, except this." Edwin was able to return to his beloved stage.

Was this just one of those strange quirks of fate? Or was there another handprint behind all of this?

When we adhere to these Spiritual Laws of Consciousness, Love, Compensation, Non-Resistance and Being, we find that our lives become rich, flowing, and full of indescribable events, much like those princes of Serendip. These spiritual laws give us peace of mind, and they also work lovingly for those around us. They give us strength and courage and happiness, and we become able to find a new dimension in our lives.

The final story from history that we will examine as an illustration of serendipity also involves a notable cast. There were two British men who had small sons. One man was a nobleman, the Duke of Marlborough, and the other was a crofter, which is an occupation similar to a sharecropper. The crofter worked some land of the Duke's, an estate that the nobleman or his family members sometimes visited on retreat.

During one visit to the estate, the nobleman's son wandered out to an area which included a peat bog. Peat bogs are exceptionally dangerous places, because the ground can suck you down and swallow you up. This boy did not seem to know any better, because he wandered right into one and very quickly realized he was in trouble. He yelled and screamed, and he felt himself being sucked down very quickly.

The crofter, who was working out in the fields, heard the distant cries and, grabbing a board, rushed to the boy's rescue. When he came to the edge of the peat bog, the crofter laid the board down and scooted gingerly across it until he reached the boy. He was slowly able to pull the boy to safety.

When the Duke of Marlborough heard about the crofter risking his own life to save his son, he called the crofter to him. The Duke said he would do anything at all for the crofter, he just had to name it. But the crofter declined, saying, "No, kind sir, I only did what I wanted to do." Yet a few years later, the crofter did approach the nobleman, and said, "What I did for your son I would have done no matter what. But since you said you would do anything for me, I now have a request. It is not for me, but for my son."

The Duke listened as the crofter explained, "I have a very bright son, sir. Here in these rural schools, he will only be able to complete the third grade. He deserves better than that, and I would like for him to be able to continue his education." The Duke agreed to the crofter's request, saying, "As long as he excels in school, I will pay for your son's tuition, housing and board."

The crofter's son, in fact, did very well in school. He went all the way to college, and from there he went on to graduate school. He even received a medical degree. The young man's name was Alexander Fleming, and he discovered penicillin.

The nobleman's son, whose life the crofter saved, grew up to become the remarkable leader of Britain, Winston Churchill. And during the bleakest hours of the Second World War, Churchill came down with double pneumonia. It was penicillin that saved his life. Churchill came back strong, and inspired his fellow countrymen to hold on through the darkness and never give up the fight. The tide of World War II forever changed. All the forces of the universe are weaving this story together. This is serendipity. This is the way life works, when we let it!

When we start looking at these stories weaving together, we begin to realize that they are not just stories out of history; they are the tapestries of our own lives as well. When we get ourselves out of the way, then God, joy, love and peace can flow through us. And they forever flow in wonderful, majestic and creative ways.

There is no place where God is not, as Nanak answered the guard when told that he blasphemed by praying with his feet toward God, "As you wish. Show me where God is not, and I shall place my feet in that direction."

God is everywhere, and by focusing ourselves on the guidance of Spirit, we will find our splendor no longer imprisoned. We have opened ourselves wholly to the nourishment that is eternally offered us by the universe. We are living in the divine flow of life, and we are supported in each and every moment.

Remember that you and everything around you is a creation of joy. Yours is a radiant being, for you *are* a child of light. Blessings on your sacred journey.

Afterword

*I love to think of nature as an unlimited
broadcasting station through which
God speaks to us every day,
every moment of our lives,
if we will only tune in.*
George Washington Carver

Oftentimes we may feel that we have tried to follow the spiritual principles discussed in this book, yet we look at our lives and think that not much has changed. There is a very good reason for this. *Spiritual growth is subtle.* Although we may feel that we are exactly the same, most likely we are not. We lack the perspective to understand just how much we have grown.

Many years ago, my friend Doug and I went to climb Mount Si near Seattle. Neither of us had ever been there before. We had been told which road to take, where to park, and where the trail began. After parking and getting our gear together, we eagerly started our hike up the trail. The trail wound up and then down through the forest. It seemed that no matter how high we climbed, we would always come back down.

After nearly five miles, Doug and I stopped and wondered if we were on the wrong trail. Maybe we had gotten on a trail that went around the mountain rather than to the summit. We asked ourselves, how far should we go on without seeing some evidence of our progress? We sat for some time and then finally decided that we would go on just a little farther. In less than half a mile, we suddenly broke out above the tree line and could see the towering peak, straight ahead. We had been progressing all along and yet without the proper perspective, we could not know how far we had come.

Let me close with two notes of encouragement for those times when it is difficult to know whether you are making any progress. *Keep to your path, and remember that you have grown more than you realize.* You will find that as you pay more attention to the details of the spiritual life, you will be responding to events and crisis in your life with a novel, radiant and serene perspective that is harmonizing with the energies of the universe. You will then find that you have unlocked the imprisoned splendor. *Let your light shine forth.*

Robert Wasner is a world traveler, and over the past 30 years has led tours to over thirty countries on six continents. If you would like to join him on one of these adventures, please call or write:

Robert A. Wasner
109 Hekili Street
Kailua, Hawaii 96734
(808) 261-7140

If you would like to order
additional copies of

The Imprisoned Splendor
Discovering Your Spiritual Self

please contact:

Malamalama Press
109 Hekili Street
Kailua, Hawaii 96734
1(808) 261-7140
fax 1(808) 254-2276

Send $10.00 per book, plus
$2.50 for shipping and
handling (.50 S & H for each
additional book).
Hawaii residents add 4%
G E Tax.

Please remit in U.S. funds.
Checks, Money Orders and Credit Cards
accepted (Mastercard or Visa only)

# of copies _____ $ enclosed _____

name _____
address _____
city _____
state _____ zip_____
phone _____

credit card: type_____exp._____
number _____

Thank You